MW00915038

SCREEN ED

your

"DRIVER'S EDUCATION" MANUAL

for smartphones

By Amy Adams, MSW
Illustrated by Hannah Mackay
Layout & Design by Lindsay Sparti
Parent's Guide by Jeannie Ondelacy Sprague, M.Ed.

Recommended for ages 11-15

To my children :
this is my love letter to you

Table of Contents

Introduction: Why You Need "Driver's Ed" for Your Smartphone

"Rules of the Road"

"Detours"

"Dead Ends"

"Ready to Hit the Road"

Introduction:
Why You Need "Driver's Ed" for Your Smartphone

Modern technology is amazing. The tiny smartphone in your hand is more powerful than NASA's whole computer system that sent the first man to the moon. Your phone can either be a tool to help you in life or a terrible master that enslaves you. Before wielding such amazing power, you must learn to properly use it.

Let's compare using your phone to driving a car. It would be foolish to hand you the keys to a car unless you had taken a driver's education course, had lots of practice with an experienced driver, and been given a license to drive. Without education and training, you might seriously hurt yourself or someone else on the road.

This manual is your "driver's education" for smartphones and can help you learn the basic rules and potential dangers of phone use. It's broken down into simple, short sections to help you become a good "driver." Like any new driver, you will make mistakes. But as you establish good digital habits, you will be able to avoid serious accidents and heartache.

RULES

of the

Road

What you need to know to:

USE YOUR SMARTPHONE SAFELY

Chapter 1:
Who You Are & Why it Matters

> "It matters not how strait the gate, How charged with punishments the scroll, I am the master of my fate, I am the captain of my soul."[1]
> -William Ernest Henley

Pop Quiz! Who turned a river to blood and unleashed 9 other plagues on a group of bad guys, received 10 commandments on stone tablets that changed the world, and led a nation of people out of slavery? Congratulations if you guessed it was **Moses**. He was one of the most influential men that has ever lived. But before he was called to be a prophet and could do all these miracles, God first told him, "I am the Lord God Almighty...and, behold, thou art my son...and I have a work for thee."[2] The Lord told him this not once, not twice, but three times in a row. Clearly the Lord needed Moses to understand who he was so he could then do great things.

CHILD OF GOD

Like Moses, you too are a child of God and have important things to do. Heavenly Father, the most powerful being and the creator of the whole universe, is the Father of your spirit. He loves you more than you can even understand. He has given you some very special gifts so that you can make it home to him.

1

GIFTS

1 **Jesus Christ.** Because of Christ, you can be forgiven when you make mistakes. His atonement gives you the power to become more than you could possibly be on your own.

2 **The Holy Ghost.** He is there to teach, protect, guide, comfort, warn, confirm, and testify. You will need his guidance to help you navigate your life's journey, including how to use a smartphone safely.

3 **AGENCY,** the ability to choose for yourself what you will do and who you will become. You get to choose your actions but you don't get to choose the consequences, so you must choose wisely. Remember that you are the master of your destiny.

AGENCY: YOUR FREEDOM TO CHOOSE. AGENCY IS THE GIFT THAT HEAVENLY FATHER HAS GIVEN EACH OF US TO MAKE CHOICES AND ACT FOR OURSELVES. WE ABSOLUTELY NEEDED AGENCY FOR THE PLAN OF SALVATION TO WORK. WITHOUT IT, WE WOULDN'T BE ABLE TO LEARN OR GROW OR FOLLOW JESUS CHRIST.

4 **Talents.** You have been given a unique set of talents. As you discover and develop your talents, they will bless your life and those around you.

Other gifts include your **body**, your **family, nature,** even your **life.**

Knowing that you are a **child of God** can help you remember to keep your eye on the prize, which is **eternal life.** A smartphone can help you use these gifts to find joy and happiness or it can distract you from doing the important things you were sent here to do.

Show what you know about
Who You Are & Why It Matters :

1. Who are you?

_____

_____

_____

_____

2. What are some of the gifts Heavenly Father has given all his children to help them on their journey home to him?

●

●

●

●

3. What are some of the unique talents Heavenly Father has given you?

●

●

●

●

Chapter 2:
The Law of Opposition

"We enjoy warmth because we have been cold. We appreciate light because we have been in darkness. By the same token, we can experience joy because we have known sadness."
— David Weatherford

CHOICES

You know that terrible feeling you have when you are about to take a test that you didn't study for? What if the smartest kid in the class (who happens to sit next to you) offered to show you all the correct answers? What would you do?

You are constantly making choices between right and wrong. If there were no evil there could be no good. This is called the Law of Opposition. You can choose God's way which is freedom and eternal life, or you can choose Satan's plan which is captivity and death. Seems like a no brainer, right? Of course you would pick freedom over being in jail! But here's the thing: **Satan is tricky**. He has to be tricky because if he told you the truth, you would never choose it.

BEWARE OF TRICKS

Satan tries to lure you by imitation. He tries to sell you a fake product, promising that it's real. He says things like, "this will make you feel good," or, "this will make you cool." He attempts to trick you by making God's commandments look foolish or convincing you that just one time won't hurt you. Satan wants the appetites and desires of your body to control you. He wants to completely control you like a puppet so that you can be as miserable as him.

Heavenly Father will help you learn to have control over your body. Each time you choose to obey God's commandments you are blessed with His Spirit and with more freedom.

God's goal = your eternal happiness

Satan's goal = your eternal misery

GOALS

A phone provides you with endless opportunities to make choices that will either help or hurt you. As you learn to reject the bad and, instead, recognize and use all the good that your phone has to offer, you will become a wise technology user.

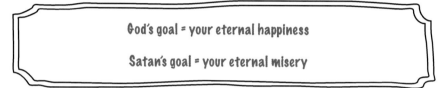

Show what you know about
The Law of Opposition:

1. Why do you think Satan has to be so tricky to fool you into making choices that will hurt you?

_____

_____

_____

_____

2. What is God's goal for you?

_____

_____

_____

_____

Chapter 3:
Danger Ahead and How to Avoid It (Your 4 Safeguards)

*"No safety,
know pain.
Know safety,
no pain."
- Unknown*

What do yield signs, danger ahead signs, stop signs, and icy road signs all have in common? Yup, you guessed it: they all keep you safe on the road. Similarly, there are four **SAFEGUARDS** that will help keep you safe while using your smartphone.

The 4 Safeguards are:

1. Seek the Spirit

2. Remember your purpose

3. Be disciplined

4. Team Up!

SAFEGUARD: STEPS TO TAKE TO PROTECT SOMEONE OR SOMETHING OR TO PREVENT SOMETHING BAD FROM HAPPENING.

Chapter 4:
Safeguard #1: Seek the Spirit

"Imagine the miracle of it! We can pray to our Heavenly Father and receive guidance and direction, be warned about dangers and distractions, and be enabled to accomplish things we simply could not do on our own. If we will truly receive the Holy Ghost and learn to discern and understand His promptings, we will be guided in matters large and small."[3]
—Russell M. Nelson

YOUR SWORD

Imagine you are a soldier living 500 years ago and have been sent into battle. Without a sword you're dead. Your sword is so important because it can be used to both attack and defend. Now fast forward to today. There is a battle raging for your soul. You need the "sword of the spirit"[4] which is the Holy Ghost, to help you cut through Satan's lies and attacks so you can defeat him.

Your phone can bring so much good into your life, but because of the Law of Opposition Satan will try to use it to hurt you. You need the Holy Ghost to warn you of danger. Learning to

11

recognize and follow the Spirit's influence will protect and guide you to safety.

To have the Spirit in your life, focus on Christ and make an effort to pray and keep the commandments. *You don't need to be perfect, just trying.* When you make mistakes you can repent and improve. If you find yourself going down the wrong path, talk to your parents and your bishop who can help you turn around and be free.

If you are using a device and something inappropriate pops up, the Spirit may **warn** you with strong feelings of **danger** and **dread**.

As you go online, there will be many things that look like truth but aren't. The Holy Ghost can help you **DISCERN** between truth and error. If something is true, He will cause you to have *good, peaceful feelings.* If it isn't true you will feel **uneasy and confused.**

> **DISCERN: COME TO KNOW OR RECOGNIZE THE DIFFERENCE BETWEEN TWO DIFFERENT THINGS, LIKE RIGHT OR WRONG, SO YOU CAN MAKE A CHOICE.**

THE STILL, SMALL VOICE

Your phone allows you access to many opinions, ideas and voices. Remember that the most important voice is the Spirit. The Spirit usually does not speak in a loud voice. More often than not he whispers in a *still, small voice* to your **heart** and your **mind**. If you constantly have your face in a screen or your earbuds in, you may be drowning out the voice of the Spirit.

Quiet time without your phone allows you more opportunities to listen to and learn from the Holy Ghost. You can use a journal to write down experiences you've had feeling the Holy Ghost. When you feel sad or lonely, you can go back and read about those experiences to remind yourself how much God loves you. If you start to do inappropriate things online, the Spirit will leave you. His departure will likely leave you feeling lost and alone.

> If you quickly learn to recognize what the absence of the Spirit feels like, you will avoid many dead end paths.

God has given you the gift of the Holy Ghost to help you. Please don't leave the present unwrapped on a shelf. Open it up and learn how to use this marvelous gift.

Show what you know about
Safeguard #1 - Seek The Spirit:

1. Share a time when you felt the Spirit. How did it feel?

_____

_____

_____

_____

2. What are some of things you can do on a daily basis to ensure that the Spirit can dwell with you?

●

●

●

●

3. What feelings might you have if the Holy Ghost is trying to warn you?

_____

_____

_____

_____

4. What feelings might you experience if the Holy Ghost departs?

_____

_____

_____

_____

14

5. What can you do to increase your ability to recognize and listen to the Spirit?

_____

_____

_____

_____

6. As you use your phone, ask yourself if what you are doing is inviting or impeding (stopping) the Spirit and his influence. How will you know the difference?

_____

_____

_____

_____

7. How might a smartphone distract you from feeling the Spirit?

_____

_____

_____

_____

8. Where will you record experiences you have had feeling the Holy Ghost?

-
-
-
-

Chapter 5:
Safeguard #2: Remember Your Purpose

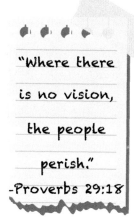

"Where there

is no vision,

the people

perish."
-Proverbs 29:18

When I first got a smartphone, I couldn't believe how often I would pick up my phone to look up something and then, hours later, I would find myself still on the phone without having accomplished my initial task. Learning to remember my purpose helped me understand that it's easy to get sucked into the black hole of wasting time and that I needed to fix the problem. This safeguard can help you too.

Every time you pick up your phone you should ask yourself two questions:

1. What is my specific purpose in using the phone right now?

2. How much time will this take?

When you have a specific purpose for using your phone, it can be a wonderful tool. Without a purpose, your phone can become a master who enslaves you.

YOUR ULTIMATE PURPOSE

God's purpose is for you to make it back to live with Him in eternal happiness. He wants you to find joy and happiness now and forever. Keep your eyes focused on the big picture as you make small daily choices with your phone and other media.

If you forget your ultimate purpose then it's easy to think that small choices don't matter. Two of Satan's biggest tricks are to make you forget that you are a child of a loving Heavenly Father and to make you believe that pleasure is the same as happiness and joy. **Don't be tricked!**

PLEASURE VS. HAPPINESS

Pleasure means the good feelings you experience when you give your body something it will enjoy. Pleasure is over quickly and runs out fast. For example, eating a donut is a pleasurable experience. Pleasure is not a bad thing every once in a while or at appropriate times, but it shouldn't be your most important goal.

Happiness is a stronger and bigger feeling. You find happiness as you keep the commandments, develop your talents, serve others, and spend time with friends and family.

Don't confuse pleasure with happiness because they really aren't the same at all! Pleasure comes from taking or getting something for yourself. Happiness comes from giving to others and thinking about more than just yourself. Happiness takes work and effort but leaves you feeling good much longer.

Your phone provides you with tons of ways to find pleasure, but true happiness is most likely found in real life. Don't waste time chasing after pleasure instead of seeking happiness.

BOREDOM IS NOT A (PURPOSE)

The average person can't go longer than 10 minutes without checking his phone, and checks it up to 150 times a day.[5] **What about you?**

Life in the digital age means that you never have to be bored because there is always a game to play, a post to like, or a video to share. Being bored can actually be a good thing. It gives your brain a break from constant information. Boredom leads to creativity. I recently left my kids home alone with the instruction that they were not to use any screens while I was gone. They got bored and decided to make cookies and lemonade. They walked down to the corner, set up shop and made $30 in an hour. Awesome! Had they been on their screens this would have never happened.

Are you picking up your phone sometimes just because you are bored? If you don't have a specific (purpose,) you are more likely to encounter inappropriate material as you casually scroll and search with no clear direction.

Next time you're bored and tempted to pick up your phone, let your imagination run wild instead. You might surprise yourself.

ENTERTAINMENT IS DESSERT

Seeking clean entertainment is not bad. Everyone deserves to chill a little and unwind. But, if you are seeking entertainment to avoid something else, then put the phone down and do what needs to be done first. Think of it like dessert. Dessert is great, but you need to eat your dinner first.

Put a time limit on entertainment **BEFORE** you start. Don't get sucked into wasting a whole day seeking entertainment.

HOW MUCH TIME WILL THIS TAKE?

When you ask yourself "How much time will this take?" before you use your phone, you are keeping yourself from wasting time and detouring from your purpose.

You, your family, and your friends can hold each other accountable for your phone use. When you see each other on your phones, ask "What is your purpose and how long will it take you?"

PUT IT DOWN!

After you accomplish your purpose in the time frame you've set aside, you need to **PUT THE PHONE DOWN**. So many teens (and adults, too) walk around holding their phones in their hands like they can't handle being apart from them. Try putting your phone in your pocket, in a backpack, or even in another room. Try not holding it for several minutes.

Remember: you're the boss of the phone!

Show what you know about
Safeguard #2 - Remember Your Purpose:

1. What are the two questions you should ask yourself every time you pick up your phone?
-
-

2. What's the difference between pleasure and happiness?

_____
_____
_____
_____

3. When should you *not* use your phone?

_____
_____
_____
_____

4. How much time per day should you spend on your phone?

_____
_____
_____
_____

5. How much time per day or per week should you spend on entertainment such as watching videos, playing games, or looking at social media?

_____
_____
_____
_____

Chapter 6:
Safeguard #3: Be Disciplined

"You will never always be motivated. You have to learn to be disciplined"
-anonymous

As human beings we are always looking for shortcuts. Most of us follow **the Law of the Least,** which means that we want to put in the least amount of effort for the same result. It also means that when given a choice between doing something hard or something easy, we almost always choose the easy way. For example, I love pineapples because they are tangy and sweet, but they are annoying to cut. So, if I come into the kitchen and can choose between a pineapple or grapes, I usually grab the grapes because they are easier even though I like pineapple better. So what's the answer to overcoming this?

It takes discipline to over-come the law of the least. Discipline is the ability to **work hard** even when the task is difficult. It is deciding to be strong instead of giving up. It's **choosing the right,** even if it's not convenient or fun.

23

YOU CAN DO HARD THINGS

Playing the piano, excelling at a sport, learning a foreign language and doing well in school all take discipline. **Michael Jordan** is considered one of the greatest basketball players of all time. But did you know that he didn't make his varsity team when he tried out as a Sophmore? From that moment he worked harder and longer than anyone else and the results speak for themselves.

Anything of value and meaning comes as a result of discipline. Think of how much discipline **Thomas Edison** had to have to invent the lightbulb. It took him 1,000 tries. That's 999 failures!

You can learn to be disciplined and make good choices about how you use technology, even though it's not always easy. This struggle is obvious when you enter a room and see that most people are sucked into their devices when they could be interacting with others.

Just because "everyone else" is doing it (ignoring the people around them, playing the latest video game for hours at a time, posting questionable pictures on social media, or looking at pornography) doesn't mean that those behaviors are okay. As you become disciplined, you will have the courage to do the right thing even if nobody else is.

Show what you know about
Safeguard #3 - Be Disciplined

1. What are some rules you will make for yourself to help you be disciplined with your phone?

-
-
-
-

2. When have you been disciplined at doing something? How did it make you feel?

_____

_____

_____

_____

3. Why is it so hard to be disciplined?

_____

_____

_____

_____

4. What are some of the benefits you can get from being disciplined with your phone?

-
-
-
-

The Grandma Rule:

Grandma is on your (team.)
If you wouldn't feel
comfortable with
Grandma seeing it, don't watch
it, read it, like it, or post it!

Chapter 7:
Safeguard #4: Team Up!

> "Alone we can
> do so little;
> together we can
> do so much."
> – Helen Keller

Have you ever been a part of a **winning team?** When I was a senior in high school I was the captain of my cross country team. My teammates and I worked hard all season and pushed each other to succeed. We were friends on and off the course. During that final race, someone tripped me and I face-planted on the ground. This had never happened to me before and I wondered how I'd ever recover from it. I knew my teammates were depending on me to do my best so, with shouts of encouragement from my coach and fellow teammates, I got up and finished the race. We won the meet that day and took home the title of State Champions. It took all 7 of us running our best as a team and supporting each other to achieve this dream and, to this day, I can still remember the sweet feeling of victory.

YOUR TEAM

Likewise, in order to establish righteous digital habits, you need a team. The most valuable members of your team are your **parents**. Other teammates can include **siblings**, other **family members**, and **trusted adults**. You are more likely to make inappropriate choices (like pornography and sexting) when you're alone. There is strength and safety in numbers.

YOUR FAMILY TECH PLAN

Together, with your team, you will create a Family Tech Plan. The plan is found at the end of this chapter. Work together as a family to fill out each section. This plan might include random spot checks, scheduled talks, and phones being kept in public family spaces and out of private spaces like bedrooms and bathrooms. Keeping your phone out of your bedroom

> It's less tempting to misuse technology when you are around other people.

also helps you get enough sleep. I work with a lot of kids who admit that they only get a few hours of sleep each night because they stay up late on their phones in their bedrooms. Then, they come to school grouchy, exhausted, and sluggish, and have a hard time paying attention in class and getting good grades.

MISTAKES HAPPEN

When you make a mistake, talk to your parents or a trusted adult. They can help you. Never let guilt, shame, or embarrassment keep you from talking about a problem you are facing with technology. Everyone makes mistakes! Problems can be resolved and you can learn and grow from your mistakes. Use your team to help you win!

Show what you know about
Safeguard #4 - Team Up!

1. Why is appropriately using technology a team effort?

_____
_____
_____
_____

2. List all the people on your team.

-
-
-
-

3. What can you do to help your family be a team?

_____
_____
_____
_____

4. Fill out your Family Tech Plan.

my family's TECHNOLOGY PLAN
Establishing Healthy Digital Habits

1. Identify technology-related [DANGERS] that could affect your family.
(pornography, cyberbullying, addiction, negative body image, predators, lack of sleep, identity theft, wasting time, disconnection from family, pressure to keep up, feelings of missing out, etc.)

2. Carefully determine what [TECHNOLOGY] you will have in your home and the public areas where those devices will be kept.
(tv, computer, dvd, XBOX, apple tv, ipad, cell phone, etc.//parents' room, devices locked when not in use, overnight charging station, etc.)

3. Determine [TECH FREE SPACES] for your family.
(bedrooms, classrooms, church. sporting events, dinner table, behind closed doors, family outings short car rides, bathrooms, etc.)

4. Determine **TECH FREE TIMES** for your family and create a **DEVICE CURFEW.**
(meal times, talking to someone, homework, driving, when parents aren't home, while practicing an instrument, when you feel bored/lonely/angry/anxious, etc.//30 min before bedtime, etc.)

5. Determine how you will **FILTER AND LIMIT** each device in your home.
(apple restrictions, parental controls, password protected, disney circle, funamo app, etc.)

6. Plan times to **MONITOR** device activity and **COMMUNICATE** with your family about technology.
(frequent conversations during car rides or mealtime, spot checks on texts and phones, occasional family discussions, routine checks of filters and controls on phones, etc.)

7. Determine how you will use technology for **GOOD.**
(thoughtful text/email/phone calls, research, uplifting social media posts, study, etc.)

Chapter 8:
What "Big Tech" Wants From You

"The thought process was, 'How do we consume as much of your time and conscious attention as possible?'"
—Sean Parker, Co-founder of Facebook

Have you ever wondered why most apps are free? How do companies make money if they are letting you have their product free of charge? Here's the secret: the more time you spend on their app, the more money they can charge companies who want to advertise there. "Free apps" might not cost you money, but they are actually charging you in something even more precious: your time and attention.

"Big Tech," the people and companies who make apps, want you to spend as much time as possible on their apps. They don't care if you sleep. They don't care if you do your homework. They don't care about the consequences you'll face, like you losing entire chunks of your life to scrolling and playing games. **They are attention vampires.** They only care about one thing: $$$.

HOW THEY SUCK YOU IN:
Here are a few examples of sneaky ways Big Tech gets you to visit their sites and then stay awhile...preferably a L-O-N-G while.

- **Autoplay** - The next video automatically plays within seconds of finishing the last one. They choose what they think you might like based on what you just viewed, keeping you hooked on watching video after video after video. They *win* because they sucked you into watching sixteen videos when you only intended to watch one. You *Lose* because you meant to go to bed early. They get more $$$ from advertisers and you get sick from lack of sleep.

- **Streaks** - Nobody wants to stop the streak. They *win* because you are constantly checking the app and sending out messages. You *Lose* because you were going to study for a test but sent out fifty messages instead.

- **Rewards** - Online games give you rewards for reaching new levels. They make it very hard for you to put the game down because you don't want to disappoint your team. They *win* because you just spent a crazy amount of time on their site. You *Lose* because you don't have time for a real job and only have virtual gold coins.

- **Notifications** - Apps send you notifications when someone comments or likes your post. Because of those notifications, you go back onto their site over and over again and spend minutes and hours you weren't planning on, scrolling through your feed. They *win* because they got you to visit their site. You *Lose* because you neglected time with your family.

- **Feeds** - Bottomless feeds (or constantly updated lists of stories, pictures, videos, etc.) make it so that you can scroll endlessly. They *win* because they got you to click on several sponsored posts. You *lose* because you spent so much time online that you didn't have time to exercise.

These are just a few of many examples. Once you begin to understand that their purpose is to get you to stay forever, you can start gaining power over them. Do you really want them telling you when to visit their sites and how long to stay? Who is in control here? Are you the master or the slave? Don't give someone else control over your time and attention.

HOW DO YOU SUCCESSFULLY AVOID TIME TRAPS?

Know your purpose and time limit before you go to the site or app. Then, be disciplined enough to stop when you hit your predetermined time limit.

Turn off notifications. This gives you the power to check the app or website on **YOUR TIME SCHEDULE, NOT THEIRS.** This keeps you in control, not them.

Be smarter than their tricks. Don't get taken!!

Show what you know about
What Big Tech Wants from You

1. Why does Big Tech want you to spend time on their apps?

_____

_____

_____

_____

2. What are some things they do to steal your time?

•

•

•

•

3. What are some things you can do to make sure that you are in charge and not your phone?

•

•

•

•

Chapter 9:
Social Skills Matter

Right now you are learning important social skills that will help you throughout your life. Some of these include making **eye contact, talking to people,** learning how to **read body language,** and **communicating** your thoughts and feelings effectively.

You are also learning how to listen and help when friends share difficult things that they are going through. This is called **EMPATHY.**

"What's not so great is that all this technology is destroying our social skills. Not only have we given up on writing letters to each other, we barely even talk to each other. People have become so accustomed to texting that they're actually startled when the phone rings. It's like we suddenly all have Batphones. If it rings, there must be danger.
   —Ellen DeGeneres

EMPATHY: THINKING ABOUT HOW OTHERS FEEL AND IMAGINING WHAT THEIR EMOTIONS WOULD FEEL LIKE EVEN IF THEY NEVER EXPLAIN THEM TO YOU.

Having a phone can make it difficult to practice good social skills. Texting and instant messaging are replacing person-to-person interaction. When you talk to someone face-to-face, the person's facial expression, tone of voice, and body language help

37

you understand her/his thoughts and feelings about whatever is being said. Texting doesn't give you these clues. Because you cannot see and hear your friends through a text message, you might not be able to really understand what they are trying to communicate. Emojis are poor substitutes for real feelings.

Texting and other online communication can be a useful and quick way of communicating. Just make sure that you also spend time talking face-to-face with your friends.

PHONE ETIQUETTE 101

Good phone **ETIQUETTE** will help you build and maintain strong relationships. Poor etiquette will cause people to think you are rude and insensitive. Here are some guidelines:

Don't bury your face in your phone when you are around other people.

ETIQUETTE: GOOD MANNERS AND BEHAVIORS THAT PEOPLE USE TO TALK TO AND INTERACT WITH EACH OTHER.

Have you ever tried to talk to someone when they had their phone in front of them? How did it make you feel? Not good, right? When you have a phone out while you're with someone, you're sending the message that the person in front of you is less important than the piece of metal and plastic in your hand. That super important text or funny meme can wait.

Real people come first.

When you are in the car with other people, talk to them. The same is true when you are at the dinner table or other social gatherings. This takes discipline, but your family and friends will be grateful.

Don't take out your phone to avoid an awkward social situation.

Did you know that 75% of all people admit to hiding behind their phones?[7] While this is very tempting, it prevents you from going outside of your comfort zone. You will eventually move out and get a job. Nobody wants to hire somebody that doesn't know how to communicate. If you avoid talking to people, how will you ever learn this skill? The more you practice, the better you will get at it.

Don't allow your phone to interrupt face-to-face interactions.

If your phone beeps at you while you are talking to someone, resist the urge to check it. Our phones trick us

comfort zone

into thinking that everything is important and needs to be checked right away.

The most important person is the one standing in front of you.

Show what you know about
Social Skills Matter

1. How does it make you feel when you are trying to talk to someone while they are constantly staring at their phone?

_____

_____

_____

_____

2. In what situations are you going to put your phone away?

●

●

●

●

3. How are you going to let people know you are more interested in them than your phone?

_____

_____

_____

_____

4. What is one way you can go out of your comfort zone?

●

40

Chapter 10:
Your Digital Footprint

"Don't say anything online that you wouldn't want plastered on a billboard with your face on it."
– Erin Bury

Your digital footprint is everything about you that you've ever done online. It's all the things that you post, everything you click on, and every website you look at.

For better or for worse, everything you do online is permanent. Once you click "send" on a text message, share a picture, give something a thumbs up or "like" sign, publish or post, it's out there for all the universe to see and you can never take it back.

Several apps claim that you can send any message or picture you want and it will just disappear after someone opens it and views it. But the truth is you lose control over how it's used, where it goes, who sees it, or what happens to your message or image once you share it online.

> Nothing online ever really disappears.
> Don't be tricked into thinking otherwise.

You might post something in the heat of the moment but later feel bad and delete it. Unfortunately, someone may have taken a screenshot of that post and shared it with thousands of viewers. **It will never go away.** Remember, everyone (schools, colleges, the government, potential employers for that job you really want) can see everything you've ever posted.

THINK AHEAD

It's now common for colleges to look at the digital footprint you have created through social media to see if you're the type of person they want at their university. For example, 10 students were supposed to start college at Harvard until the university found out those students had created very inappropriate memes on Facebook. Harvard decided not to let those students in at all.[8]

Your future employers will also be looking at your digital footprint before hiring you. Sometimes, they'll want to see more than just your profile, like one woman who wanted to work for the FBI. The people interviewing her asked to see every single comment, picture, and post she'd ever put on social media.

> Stop and think before you post.

People will be able to follow your online trail for the rest of your life. What they find is up to you.

Show what you know about
Your Digital Footprint

1. In 10 years from now, what will the world know about you if they Google your name?

_____

_____

_____

_____

2. How will your digital footprint show that you know who you are and what your ultimate purpose is?

_____

_____

_____

_____

3. What should you do before you post?
-
-
-
-

Learn how to:
AVOID DETOURS IN YOUR LIFE

Chapter 11:
Distraction & the Myth of Multitasking

"To do two things at once is to do neither."
—Publilius Syrus

Raise your hand if you want the dentist who pulls your teeth to have watched Netflix during all his classes in dental school. For the sake of your smile, you'd better hope that he focused on what his professor was saying.

If you look around, you will notice people trying to accomplish more than one thing at a time. People text while they drive, look at social media during class, do homework while they watch TV, etc. Everyone that multitasks thinks they are good at it. But here's the secret:

> NOBODY can multitask.

Your brain can't concentrate on two things at once. When you toggle back and forth between two tasks, you will do a worse job at both tasks.[9]

You might be tempted to leave your phone out while you are doing homework, which will be a huge distraction. **Put your phone away** while you are using your brain for important tasks.

Here's some more things you can do with your phone to help you avoid getting distracted by all the bells, rings, and whistles.

> Silence it
> Do Not Disturb mode
> Airplane mode
> Turn it off
> Turn off notifications
> Have a parent 'babysit' it

Remember that it will take a lot of discipline to stay focused on your purpose at hand and not fall into the trap of letting your phone distract you. But as you learn to do this, your life will feel so much more manageable. You'll be in control of your phone instead of it controlling you.

Show what you know about
Distraction & the Myth of Multitasking

1. When are times that you are tempted to multitask?

_____

_____

_____

_____

2. List some things that you can do with your phone so that you won't get distracted.

•

•

•

•

Chapter 12:
Texting

"Texting is a brilliant way to miscommunicate how you feel, and misinterpret what other people mean."
— Stanley Behrman

Texting is a quick way to communicate. It can be a wonderful tool but there are some things to be careful about.

 Never text while you are driving!

 If you wouldn't say it to someone's face, don't text it to them.

 Never apologize over text without apologizing in real life. It's important to say sorry in person, that way the person can see that you really are sorry and you can sense how he or she took the apology.

 Remember the Grandma Rule. If your text was read out loud in front of Grandma, how would you feel? If you'd be embarrassed or ashamed, then don't send it.

5 Text only at appropriate times and places. No texting at church or during classes at school. Most texts are not emergencies and can wait until more appropriate times.

6 No texting late at night or early in the morning. Remember your phone's bedtime that you decided in the Family Tech Plan.

7 No one needs to know that you are about to take a shower or change into your swimsuit or anything else you wouldn't do in front of the person.

8 If you need to discuss something long or difficult, do it face to face. It's important for you to learn how to talk about hard things instead of taking the easy way out.

9 Don't be lazy and text someone who is physically near you.

10 Don't text someone while talking to someone else in real life. This is rude.

11 Never swear or use vulgar or sexual language.

12 Never feel obligated to immediately reply to texts. Sometimes you have more important things to do.

If a group text starts to go down a path you don't feel comfortable with, opt out immediately.

Never text a naked or revealing picture of yourself. (We'll talk more about this later on.)

Don't break up with someone by texting.

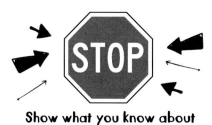

Show what you know about
Texting

1. What are some places where it would be inappropriate for you to text?

_____
_____
_____
_____

2. Give some examples of how you can use texting to help someone.

_____
_____
_____
_____

3. List 3 things you will never text.

-
-
-

Chapter 13:
Social Media

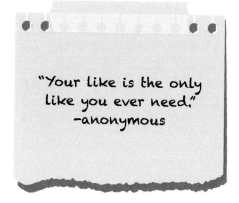

"Your like is the only like you ever need."
-anonymous

What's your "Relationship Status" with social media?

☐ Single

☐ In a healthy relationship with established boundaries and expectations

☐ In a toxic relationship - Can't go for longer than 5 minutes without checking in

☐ It's complicated

Billions of people use social media. It can be fun, but spending too much time on it can leave you feeling lonely and sad. Here's how to create a healthy relationship with it.

AGE REQUIREMENT
According to the law, users must be at least 13 years old to have a social media account. If someone younger than 13 has an account, it's because they have lied about their age. Your parents will decide what age they think is appropriate for you to have social media.

HIGHLIGHTS

Despite what you might think, social media does not show real life. Nobody's life is as perfect as it appears on your screen. People want to post things that others will like, so they usually post only the most exciting things that happen. Remember this as you scroll. When you post, try to show more than just the highlights.

Before you post, ask yourself if the picture represents *your real life*. If your room is always messy but you post a picture of the one time you cleaned it, say that.

COMPARE = DESPAIR

Social media can feel like a never-ending game of comparing your "worst self" to someone else's "best self" which can make you feel terrible.

As you scroll through the feed you might see that a lot of your friends travel to exotic locations, have expensive clothes, or drive fancy cars. You might wonder why you don't have all these things and forget about all the good stuff you do have going on in your life. When you feel like this, challenge yourself to list 5 things you are grateful for.

Pay attention to how you feel when you're reading through your friends' posts. Don't be afraid to unfollow accounts that make you feel like you're not enough, jealous, angry, or annoyed.

PRESSURES!!!

Because so many people only post perfect-looking pictures of their perfect-looking life, you can feel pressure to also have a perfect life.

Social media can create the pressure to always be "on." It's like being on a stage 24/7. How exhausting! You are always thinking about the next picture you will post instead of enjoying the moment.

This pressure can make you feel **ANXIOUS.** Did you know that some people spend hours creating the perfect post? Don't be one of those people.

THE TRUTH ABOUT LIKES

Let's pretend you're parched and you grab a cup so you can take a drink. You reach out and ask for some water but, instead of pouring water into your cup, people put a bunch of glittery heart stickers all over the outside. The cup looks shiny and fancy and, for a moment, you feel

ANXIOUS: WHEN YOUR BODY REACTS TO FEELING WORRIED, NERVOUS, OR FEARFUL BY BECOMING SWEATY, GETTING A HEADACHE, OR FEELING SICK TO YOUR STOMACHE. THIS EMOTION IS NORMAL AND CAN BE HELPFUL IN PROTECTING YOU FROM ACTUAL DANGER. ANXIETY IS WHEN YOU HAVE THESE FEARFUL FEELINGS ALL THE TIME BUT THERE IS NO REAL DANGER.

special that people thought of you. But your cup is still empty. There's no water in it for you to take a drink! When people "like" your posts on social media, it's as if they were putting a glittery heart sticker on the outside of you but you're not ever getting filled on the inside. The only way to "fill your cup" is by "pouring" in things that make you feel happy such as **spending time with friends, helping someone in need, doing a hobby,** or **being creative.** Do things to fill your cup, not just to make yourself feel shiny.

You might think that the more "likes" you get, the more important you are, but this isn't true. "Likes" do not equal friendship in real life, only in a virtual world.

Unfortunately, some people post sexy pictures of themselves because they think that this will get them more "likes." Never post anything sexy, EVER!!! Doing this to get "likes" sends the message that you think your value is found only in the way you look. Don't reduce your value to just your body. In the end, how much you like yourself will always be more important than how many "likes" you get. Be confident in how awesome you are.

LIVE YOUR LIFE
Social media can trap you into a virtual existence. You can become consumed in "stalking" other people's lives. Don't let FOMO (Fear of Missing Out) make you miss out on your own life. Learn to enjoy your life by doing things you love, because you only get one life.

REAL FRIENDSHIPS?
Social media is a fun way to know what's going on in people's lives, but knowing what's going on and feeling close to someone are two very different things. There are so many things about a person that you will never learn from social media. Real friendships take time, face-to-face talking, and work. Spend time with your friends in real life, don't just scroll their feeds.

CONSTANT ATTENTION-SEEKING
Social media promotes an "all-about-me" attitude. People post crazy amounts of selfies to get praise and attention. The truth is that the sooner you learn that it's not all about you, the better your life will be. When your time is spent focused on yourself, it's really hard to show love and concern for others.

REMEMBER WHO YOU ARE!
Be the same person online as you are in real life.

BE MODEST
No one likes a bragger. You might be a really fast runner, but you don't need to post every time you win a race. Have the discipline to

be **MODEST.** Being modest would mean thinking about how those race-winning posts might make others feel. It's fine to occasionally post about your accomplishments, just make sure it's not the only thing you post.

> **MODEST:** NOT DRAWING TOO MUCH ATTENTION TO YOURSELF TO SHOW OFF. BEING MODERATE. THE OPPOSITE OF BRAGGING.

BE WELL-ROUNDED

Post a variety of different things. You are a well-rounded person with lots of hobbies, interests, friends and family. Let your social media feed show that.

THINK KINDNESS FIRST

Never post anything that makes fun of other people. It's OK to make fun of yourself, but never do it to someone else. Likewise, never make any comments on social media that are hurtful or mean. Always be kind.

BE WISE

Turn off **LOCATION SERVICES** *and* **GEOTAGGING.** Nobody needs to know where you are in real time.

Don't accept "friend" requests or follow someone you don't know in real life.

> **LOCATION SERVICES:** WHEN APPLE (OR WHATEVER KIND OF PHONE YOU HAVE) AND OTHER APP COMPANIES USE YOUR PHONE TO KNOW WHERE YOU'RE AT SO THEY CAN RECOMMEND STORES YOU CAN SHOP AT NEARBY OR PLACES CLOSE TO YOU WHERE YOU CAN EAT.

If you want to follow a public figure, talk to your parents first. Ask yourself if the message they are sending is appropriate and makes you a better person. If you are unsure, the Spirit can help you recognize if the messages are helpful or harmful.

Turn off notifications. You don't need to be informed every time someone likes or comments on your posts. Be in control of how often you go on social media because it can suck your time.

Don't over-post. Nobody needs to know every detail of your life. Over-posting will annoy people.

USE IT FOR GOOD

While scrolling through your feed, if you notice that a friend or family member is facing a difficult situation reach out to the person in real life.

Use social media to share goodness. Be uplifting and optimistic.

You are an amazing person with unique talents and abilities. If you are always looking for others to tell you that you're awesome, you will lead a very sad and lonely life. Don't fall into the trap of using social media to make yourself feel important. You are already awesome.

Checklist Before I Post:

-Does this post show who I really am?
-Does this post show that I respect my body?
-Am I bragging? Would other people
think I was bragging?
-Have I already posted something
like this recently?
-Would this post hurt someone's feelings?
-Does this post represent my real life?
-Would Grandma approve of this post?

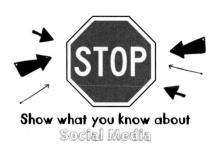

Show what you know about
Social Media

1. How often and for how long will you check social media?

_____

_____

_____

_____

2. How many posts do you think are appropriate in the space of a week?

•

3. What will you do if you find yourself posting as a way to prove your worth? What could you do instead to feel special?

_____

_____

_____

_____

4. If people only knew you from what you posted, what would they think about you?

_____

_____

_____

_____

5. What do you think is a good guideline about selfies?

_____

_____

_____

_____

60

Chapter 14:
Video Games

"Video games ruined my life. Good thing I have 2 extra lives."
—Unknown

A few years ago, a teenage boy was hospitalized for severe dehydration because he had played video games for 4 days straight.[10] There are lots of stories of people who are so addicted to gaming that they would rather pee in a bottle than get up and use the bathroom. Some kids play up to 16 hours a day. In one extreme case, a 19-year-old cut off his own hand because he was so desperate to stop gaming.[11] What's going on?

Here's what you need to know so that you can make responsible decisions about gaming.

ADDICTIVE ON PURPOSE

It's no accident that video games are so addictive. The flashy, colorful, fast-paced movement combined with rewards and advancements to new levels all make it really hard to want to put down the game. The video game industry makes billions of dollars a year. The more time you spend playing, the more money they make. They don't care about your life; they only care about making $$$.

DESSERT NOT DINNER

Video games can waste your time when you should be doing other things. Only use them for dessert--just a small amount--when you have finished needed tasks. Even games like BitLife or Cup Pong that seem to not take a lot of time can add up.

ALTERNATE REALITY

Video games offer an escape from reality. They transport you from your not-so-perfect-life into a fantasy world. But trying to escape your problems will only make those problems worse. One young man said that he started playing video games because he was lonely and didn't want to think about his problems. He wished he had never started because he became addicted and dropped out of school.

RATED WHAT?

Some video games are violent or have other inappropriate content. Even watching fake violence can make you feel less empathetic or caring towards people in real life. In fact, soldiers often train for battle by playing video games for this reason. As you seek the Spirit, he will help you recognize when something is inappropriate through uneasy feelings.

RULER OF THE WORLD?

Video games can make you feel like the king of the world. As you reach new levels and improve your skills you might feel really awesome. But the problem is that these skills don't help you achieve anything in the real world. It's only by participating in real world activities that you earn real world accomplishments. Remember your purpose!

WATCH YOUR WALLET

Video games can convince you to spend real money for virtual bling. Be careful about what video game items you spend your money on. It might seem like a good idea in the moment, but what are you really getting for it?

IMAGINE THIS!

When you play video games, you are participating in a game imagined by someone else. People who play a lot of video games tend to think less creatively because they are allowing someone else to imagine things for them. Unplug often so that you can put your creativity to good use. You might be surprised at what your creativity inspires you to make or do.

GET TOGETHER

Although it might be fun to occasionally play online with your friends, remember that you will be happiest when you are physically with other people. Talking to someone through a headset is just not the same as being with them in real life. Do fun things with your friends besides just playing video games. You'll make great memories and have better friendships this way.

STAY HEALTHY

Video games can be harmful to your physical health. It's not good for your body to sit for long periods of time. You need lots of physical activity throughout the week to stay healthy. When you don't get enough movement you can get dehydrated, gain weight, and feel sluggish. Find a physical activity that gets you outside and makes you feel happy.

BE WISE

Video games that have live chat (or other messages) can be dangerous. If you are playing with someone you don't know, please be careful. Many people with very bad intentions try to befriend kids on video games.

Show what you know about
Video Games

1. Make a list of all the video games you play. (Don't forget to include small games that you might play for only 5 minutes at a time.)

-
-
-
-

2. When and how long will you play video games? Will you play every day or only on certain days?

_____

_____

_____

_____

3. What tasks will you finish each day before playing any type of game? Examples might be homework, chores, and exercise.

_____

_____

_____

_____

4. What is your family rule about chatting with people you don't know while playing video games?

_____

_____

_____

_____

DEAD ENDS

Learn why cyberbullying, pornography, and sexting all lead to dead ends.

 *Learn how to:*

Identify – RECOGNIZE THE PROBLEM

Act – DO SOMETHING ABOUT IT

Level Up! – EVALUATE SO YOU CAN DO BETTER

Chapter 15:
Cyberbullying

> I would rather be a little nobody, than to be an evil somebody.
> -Abraham Lincoln

Before the internet, if a kid bullied you at school, at least you could be safe at home. Now, thanks to technology, that bully can follow you everywhere you go. One grieving brother of a teen who had recently committed suicide posted, "In today's age, bullies don't push you into lockers, they cower behind user names and fake profiles from miles away constantly berating and abusing good, innocent people." [12]

Up to **59%** of kids have been cyberbullied, and **90%** of kids have seen someone cyberbullied [13]

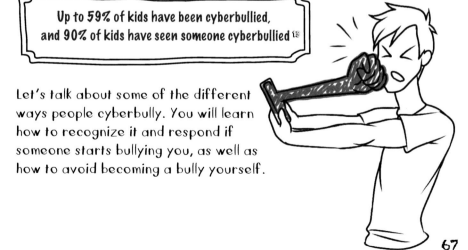

Let's talk about some of the different ways people cyberbully. You will learn how to recognize it and respond if someone starts bullying you, as well as how to avoid becoming a bully yourself.

IDENTIFY
BULLIES DO THIS...

Post **rude**, embarrassing, or **cruel comments** about someone.

Bambi's friend Thumper the Rabbit was right: **if you can't say anything nice, don't say anything at all.** If you wouldn't say it to the person in front of his or her face, don't post it. You might think you're trying to be funny, so a good rule of thumb before you post is to ask yourself how you would feel if that comment was sent to you? If there is any doubt in your mind, don't do it.

Hide behind a **fake** or anonymous **profile** or username. You are more likely to say mean things when you are anonymous because you think nobody will find out that it's you. If you find yourself wanting to do this, just don't.

Threaten to **hurt** or **kill** someone or tell them to kill themselves.

Post or forward a **mean**, or embarrassing, or a naked/semi-naked **picture, meme, GIF,** or **video online.**

Talk trash about people online. Remember that someone could screenshot the conversation and send it elsewhere, creating hurt feelings and damaging friendships.

> **Pause before you post**

Is it **kind?** Is it **true?** Is it **necessary?** Would Grandma approve? If not, don't do it!

ACT
THINGS YOU CAN DO TO GIVE BULLIES LESS ACCESS TO YOU...

1. Spend **less time** online.

Did you know that teens who spend 3 hours or more per day on social networks are significantly more likely to be cyberbullied? The more time you spend online, the more risk you have of someone bullying you.

2. Never share your **password** with anyone except your parents.

Today's friend might be tomorrow's enemy. If you give your friend your password and then get into a fight, your friend may get into your account to post mean or hateful things about you.

3. Don't give out too much information **(TMI).** Sharing too many personal details can give cyberbullies more ammo to use against you.

WHAT YOU CAN DO IF YOU ARE BEING CYBERBULLIED...

1. Don't let it get to you.

Don't give them **power** over you. One girl who was continually cyberbullied said that she had to learn not to let their hateful words make her feel bad about herself. She decided that she wasn't going to believe the horrible things they said about her.

2. Don't respond to cyberbullies.

Have you ever noticed that when you throw a tiny crumb to a seagull at the beach, suddenly you have a million seagulls pecking at you looking for food? It's the same online. If you feed the cyberbully by responding, you are only making him bigger, stronger, and more powerful. Responding to a cyberbully also gives concrete proof that he has succeeded in hurting you. The best thing you can do is to **ignore** cyberbullies and block them from your account.

3. Take a break.

If someone is continually harassing you online, you might need to take a **break** from that particular app. A young girl I know is currently being cyberbullied on social media but refuses to get off the app. Instead, she is trying to transfer to a new school. Taking a break might not feel fair to you since you are the one getting hurt, but by completely removing yourself from the arena, you will make it much harder for them to torment you.

4. Don't suffer in silence!

You might feel embarrassed about talking to your parents or trusted adult about being cyberbullied, but please know that they will help and support you. Remember, they're on your team.

Level Up!

1. What can help you avoid cyberbullies?

_____
_____
_____
_____

2. How will you avoid being a cyberbully?

_____
_____
_____
_____

Chapter 16:
Pornography

Pornography (or porn) is pictures, videos, cartoons, or other materials of people with little to no clothing on or people having sex. Porn is designed to make you feel sexually excited. It tempts you to use your God given desires for easy pleasure instead of real happiness.

"Put on the whole armour of God, that ye may be able to stand against the wiles of the devil. Stand therefore, having your loins girt about with truth."
-Ephesians 6:11 14

Loins refer to the parts of your body that are used to create children. In learning the truth about God's Law of Chastity, you can arm yourself with the ability to fight off Satan's lies and temptations.

The truth is that you are a child of God. As part of the Plan of Happiness, you chose to come to earth to gain a body so that you could progress towards eternal happiness. After the Lord created the earth, He commanded Adam and Eve to have children. He gave them (and you) the power to create bodies for his spirit children. We call this power procreation or sex.

It's an amazing gift that God has given you.

Because this **power** is so important to His plan for your happiness, He gave you rules regarding its use.

> "Physical intimacy between husband and wife is beautiful and sacred. It is ordained of God for the creation of children and for the expression of love between husband and wife. God has commanded that sexual INTIMACY be reserved for marriage." -For the Strength of Youth [14]

God has also given you sexual desires. These desires are good when used in the right way at the right time. One of the biggest tests of earth life is learning how to control your body and all the things it wants to experience, including sex. It takes a lot of self-control and discipline to teach your spirit to be the boss of your body. Someday you will have the privilege of creating a family and you will experience true joy.

INTIMACY: A PERSONAL OR PRIVATE CLOSE RELATIONSHIP WITH SOMEONE WHERE YOU ARE SHARING THINGS JUST BETWEEN THE TWO OF YOU.

Satan's whole purpose is to destroy your eternal happiness and progression. He wants you to be **miserable** like him. It's no wonder why he has taken this beautiful power and righteous desire and twisted them for dark and evil uses. The selfish and improper use of sex will always result in **unhappiness** and **misery** no matter how much the world tries to convince you otherwise. Pornograpy is just one of the many ways the purpose of sex has been twisted.

Satan will try to convince you that there is no harm in giving in to inappropriate sexual things like pornography. But he is lying.

PORN IS A TERRIBLE MONSTER

Pornography is a Liar. Porn tells you that the most important thing you have to offer someone is your body. This is a lie. You have so much more to offer. You are a **Child of God** full of unique **talents** and **personality** (remember the list of your talents that you made in Chapter 1). Porn tells you that you can be happy by taking, without giving anyone love in return. It is LUST pretending to be love. Intimacy is about love and being connected to a real person.

LUST: ONLY LOOKING TO SATISFY YOUR OWN BODY'S WANT OF SEX; A SUPER POWERFUL CRAVING FOR SEX.

Pornography is selfish. It tries to get you to think of only yourself and your own body's wants. Pornography makes it difficult for you to empathize and care about others because you are only thinking of yourself.

Pornography is a fake. It does not show real bodies. Generally speaking, the bodies shown in porn are airbrushed or made to look better through surgery. People in real life do not have bodies that look like that. Porn sets up unrealistic ideas about how people should look.

SEXIST: DISCRIMINATING AGAINST, OR THINKING SOMEONE IS LESS THAN, FOR BEING A FEMALE.

Pornography is SEXIST. Most pornography shows men as powerful and women as submissive, weak, and inferior. In contrast, God teaches us that men and women are equal in His eyes.

75

Pornography is a **thief.** It steals the hearts and minds of the people who use it. It demands more and more time, attention, and money. It takes and takes and takes, robbing you of real-life relationships.

Pornography is a **destroyer** of relationships. It breaks down trust and hope. Porn kills love.

"It is like a raging storm, destroying individuals and families, utterly ruining what was once wholesome and beautiful." [15]
-Gordon B. Hinckley

Pornography makes you **lonely.** Real life relationships provide happiness, companionship, and belonging. A pornographic relationship with your screen will leave you feeling empty, alone, angry, embarrassed and ashamed.

coward   hijacker   sexist

fraud

thief   destroyer

selfish

liar

Pornography is a **hijacker.** It is super addictive and hijacks or takes over your brain. You have two parts to your brain, the "thinking brain" and the "feeling brain." When the feeling brain sees pornography, it hijacks the thinking part of your brain, and makes it hard for you to make good choices and control your impulses.

Pornography **hurts** you physically. It makes it difficult for your body to have a sexual response to a real person, leaving you unable to have sex in real life.

Pornography **REPELS** the Holy Ghost and will cause him to leave you.

Pornography is a **coward.** It hides and thrives in dark and secret places. It tries to lure you when you are alone. How long would pornography survive if it were only viewed in broad daylight in front of other people, like your grandma? Not very long! This is why it is so important that **your phone does not go in your bedroom, especially at night when you are alone.**

Porn is everywhere. It's on billboards, on the cover of magazines, on store windows, and all over the internet. Unfortunately, even if you are not seeking it out, pornography will find you. You must **prepare** so you can fight against pornography.

When confronted with pornography, how you choose to respond makes all the difference.

An example of a good response is the Old Testament story of **Joseph** who was sold as a slave by his brothers. Because of Joseph's goodness, he was made an overseer in Potiphar's house. Potiphar's wife began to notice Joseph and asked him to have sex with her. He refused her time after time. It is important to remember that Joseph did not go looking for this, rather she came to him temping him over and over again. But Joseph was firm in his desire to do what was right. One day she grabbed ahold of his clothing and he immediately **fled** the scene. He got away from her as fast as he could.

77

Now let's contrast this story with that of **David**, the same one who killed Goliath. David was a good man who also found himself in a difficult situation. One evening, he went up to his roof and there saw a beautiful woman named Bath-sheba bathing. Instead of running away from the temptation, like Joseph did, he let his bodily appetites take control of him. He ended up having sex with her. She was married, and to make matters even worse, he arranged for her husband to be killed in battle.

Both Joseph and David faced temptation. Their responses forever shaped their lives. In the moment of temptation, Joseph fled, while David let himself give in to the temptation. David's poor decision led to other poor decisions.

When faced with the temptation to view pornography, will you flee or give in? Decide now to flee and the Lord will always help you escape, even when it seems impossible.

The best defense for pornography is a good offense. Study the steps in the following plan so you are ready when pornography attacks.

IDENTIFY
RECOGNIZE IT - WHAT TO DO WHEN YOU SEE PORN

When you are faced with a pornographic image, tell yourself, "This is pornography!" By recognizing pornography and choosing to act, you are allowing your thinking brain to be in charge of your feeling brain.

Remember that the Holy Ghost will help you to identify pornography. The Spirit is your "sword" which will help you cut through all of

Satan's lies to see the truth. The Spirit will warn you every time there's danger.

Be aware that you are more likely to be tempted by pornography when you are feeling strong negative emotions like fear, anxiety, anger, or sadness. People turn to pornography to soothe their emotions because, once the pleasure part of the brain is switched on, all other emotions are blocked out by this strong feeling. Trying to comfort yourself by watching pornography is like trying to make yourself feel better by taking poison.

ACT
NOW'S THE TIME TO FLEE

1. **Shut off** your screen immediately.

2. **Walk away.** Get out of there. Physically remove yourself from the temptation. You can discipline yourself so that this becomes easy to do.

3. **Tell someone.** Remember that you have a team and they are there to help you. You never, ever need to be embarrassed about pornography. Your parents and/or trusted adult will help you.

4. **Make a change.** Don't return to the site of the pornography. You may need to remove certain apps from your phone.

> You can stand strong when confronted with pictures or videos that tempt you to forget your identity and purpose. Pray for this ability every day, and you will receive help from above to "quench all the fiery darts of the wicked." [16]

1. When and to whom will you turn your phone in each night?

2. Name 4 of the characteristics of pornography that make it a terrible monster.
*
*
*
*

3. Which trusted adult will you talk to when you see pornography?

4. Where will you not use your phone or other screens? Remember, pornography thrives in dark private places.

5. What emotions or situations might make you more of an easy target for temptation?

_____
_____
_____
_____

6. What will you do when you see pornography?

_____
_____
_____
_____

7. What will you do when a friend or someone around you shows your something pornographic?

_____
_____
_____
_____

8. How will you feel about your-self after viewing pornography?

-
-
-
-
-
-

How will you feel about yourself if you resist pornography?

-
-
-
-
-
-

Chapter 17:
Sexting

> "Self respect, self worth, and self love all start with self. Stop looking outside of yourself for your value."
> – Rob Liano

IDENTIFY
SEXTING MEANS TEXTING SEXY OR NAKED PICTURES, VIDEOS, OR MESSAGES.

This is happening with kids all across the country. So what's the big deal?

send noodz

Remember who you are and what your (purpose) is. You are a **child of God** and are so much **more than your body**. You have talents, personality, intelligence, and a sense of humor. Your sexuality is also an important part of who you are and is a gift from God. If you participate in sexting you are misusing that special gift and treating yourself like an object to get attention.

> You are a person, not an object.

Satan will try and **trick** you into thinking that it's no big deal because all the kids around you are doing it. He will tell you that your value is tied to how sexy people think you are. He will whisper to you that this will make people like you or make you powerful. But this is all a lie. He will conveniently leave out the fact that sexting will make you feel cheap, hollow, and disrespected. It is demeaning to treat yourself or other people as sex objects. People are so much deeper and more complex than that.

Did you know that it is a crime to sext a picture of yourself or someone else?[17] Did you know that you can go to jail for this behavior? It is called possession or distribution of child pornography.

Remember that once you send a picture of yourself you **cannot control** where it goes. That person that you think really likes you may forward it to someone else and then someone else and on and on. Many kids end up in tears because the naked picture they thought was only going to be seen by one person ended up being seen by the whole school.

You can choose your **actions** but you have no control over the **consequences**. Please respect yourself by choosing not to sext.

ACT
To be very clear: DO NOT EVER SEND A NAKED OR SEMI-NAKED PICTURE OF YOURSELF.

If you wouldn't send it to your grandma, don't send it.

Level Up!

1. What will you do if someone asks you for a naked picture?

_____

_____

_____

_____

2. What will you do if someone sexts you?

_____

_____

_____

_____

3. What should the consequences be if your parents find out that you are sexting?

_____

_____

_____

_____

Chapter 18:
Sexual Predators

"Be careful....not all are what they seem. Some people pretend to be the beach but are actually quicksand."
—Steve Maraboli

One of my friends told me a scary story about her teenage daughter. The girl was online and started chatting with some boy she had never met before. She thought they were the same age. It was fun at first but then he started asking her to take off her clothes in front of her web camera. It turned out this person was not a teenager; he was a grown adult and a sexual predator.

Most people in the world are good. However, there are people who try to sexually take advantage of or exploit others, using them for their own purpose. A sexual predator tries to **lure** the victim into some sort of sexual contact. Kids and teenagers (both girls and boys) are often targets for these disgusting people. 1 in 7 kids that go online has been sexually solicited or approached online. [18]

IDENTIFY
RED FLAGS

If an adult you know starts to take an unusual amount of interest in you, this is a red flag. No adult should be as interested in you as your parents are. Adults should be interested in adults, not teenagers and children. It might seem flattering at first, but it's a sign of possible trouble.

Remember that people can **pretend** to be anyone online. So that person who says she is a 12 year old girl might actually be a creepy 45 year old man. If someone you don't know tries to engage in any kind of messaging or chatting with you, **DO NOT CONVERSE WITH THAT PERSON,** no matter how harmless the person may seem.

If you get a weird feeling about someone online, it's the Spirit trying to warn you. Remember that he is there to help you, so listen to him. Talk to your parents and "teammates" about it so they can help you.

One of the tricks predators use is promising you their **love, affection,** or **money** if you send them a sexual picture or video.

ACT

1. Never agree to meet someone in real life that you only know online. Remember only talk to people you already know in real life to prevent this from happening.

2. Don't share too many personal details. Even though your accounts will be private, don't **overshare** information. Never post your address or whereabouts. Post about vacations and events after, not during them.

3. Be careful about playing video games with people you do not know. You and your team should come up with a family rule about this.

4. Never take, send, or post naked or semi-naked pictures of yourself
88

or anyone else. Do not text or email them even to just one person; do not post them on social media; do not put them anywhere online.

5. Never use **sexually explicit** or aggressive language online. Never create a username of any kind that has anything about sex in it. Sexual predators may interpret this behavior as your willingness to connect sexually with them.

6. Never "friend" or text anyone you don't know **IRL (in real life).** It doesn't matter if someone is a friend of a friend or seems like a really nice person. Really "nice" people can be capable of terrible things.

7. Keep all social media accounts **private.** This way only people you know can see your posts.

Level Up!

1. To avoid sexual predators, list 4 things you will never do.

-
-
-
-

2. What will you do if you feel uneasy about someone online?

Chapter 19:
What To Do When You're Feeling "Meh"

> "You have to fight through some bad days to earn the best days of your life."
> - Anonymous

BAD DAYS

Everyone has terrible, horrible, no good, very bad days. Like the time in 7th grade when I found out that the boy I was in love with was in love with my friend. Or how about when I lost my expensive new jacket after only wearing it once. Or when my brother made me so mad I cracked an egg on his head and then I got in trouble. Yup, **bad days happen;** they're a part of life.

There are times when you will feel sad, angry, stressed, afraid, tired, lonely, or miserable, or maybe a combination of several of these emotions. One of the biggest lessons in life is learning how to deal with your negative emotions.

FACE YOUR FEELINGS

Do you remember the children's song, "Going on a Bear Hunt?" While the kids are searching for a bear, they come across many obstacles. Each time they face a new problem they say "can't go over it, can't go under it, we've got to go through it." Life is like that bear hunt song. You will face **hard things** and you will have to choose how to deal with them. When you try to go over, under, or around the problems, you will not be very successful in reaching your destination. You have to **face your feelings head on** so you can get through them instead of trying to avoid them. Many people try to avoid them or run away from them but that does nothing to help the problem.

When you feel terrible, it's tempting to want to turn to your screen for comfort. You may just want to be distracted so you don't have to think about your problems. But here's the thing:

> **You are more likely to make bad choices using your technology when you are feeling low. These choices will leave you feeling worse, instead of better.**

For example, let's say you are feeling pretty lonely one day so you decide to scroll through social media. All you see on your feed is happy people doing fun things without you. Now you feel even more lonely. Or what about if you had a big fight with your best friend during school and you were so angry in that moment that you sent a group message to a bunch of people trash-talking your friend? Afterwards, you felt **terrible** but since you had already clicked "send" in the heat of the moment it was too late.

You might be **tempted** to look at pornography when you are having a bad day because the sensations you feel while viewing pornography block out all other negative emotions. But right after you stop watching it you feel worse, not better.

ADDICTIONS happen when people use substances (such as drugs or alcohol) or behaviors (such as gambling or pornography) in hopes that their pain will lessen or go away. It doesn't work. These things are dead-end solutions and only bring pain and sorrow into your life. Remember, the trick is learning how to face negative emotions head on and learn skills that help you ultimately feel better instead of worse. So, what can you do to not fall into these traps?

IDENTIFY

The first thing you can do is **accept** that sometimes bad days happen. Nobody is spared hard times. When you are having a hard time, **admit** it to yourself. Identify what it is you're feeling.

ADDICTIONS: AN ADDICTION IS AN INABILITY TO STOP DOING SOMETHING (SUCH AS DRUGS, ALCOHOL, GAMBLING, OR PORNOGRAPHY) EVEN THOUGH IT CAUSES YOU GREAT HARM. THE WORD CAME TO US FROM ANCIENT ROME. BEING "ADDICTED" MEANT THAT YOU WERE A SLAVE. FOR EXAMPLE, WHEN SOMEONE COULDN'T PAY A DEBT HE WAS ENSLAVED OR "ADDICTED".

ARE YOU: sad, lonely, anxious, disappointed, **angry, jealous,** worried, tired, **crabby,** irritated, upset, **thirsty,** hungry, **bored,** miserable, **rejected, frustrated,** ashamed, embarrassed, **OR SOMETHING ELSE?**

By **acknowledging** your feelings, you can learn to take control of your behavior so that you don't let your negative emotions decide for you what you'll do.

Once you've identified your feelings, the next step is to figure out which negative feelings make you want to soothe yourself with technology. One young man acknowledges that he is more likely to be a cyberbully when he is angry. Another young man admits that he is tempted to view pornography when he is worried and anxious. Another girl spends hours on social media when she is feeling lonely.

There is **no shame** in being honest with yourself about what emotions are red flags for you. You can't help yourself if you aren't honest about your weak areas. By honestly acknowledging your **triggers,** you can **choose a better response**.

ACT
1. EAT, DRINK WATER, AND/OR SLEEP
There are times when you might be feeling "meh" simply because you are hungry, thirsty, or tired. When this is the case, take care of your physical needs. Every day you should make sure you are eating right, drinking enough water and getting enough sleep at night. A good night's rest can do **wonders** for your mood.

2. MOVE YOUR BODY
When you exercise, your body produces a chemical which causes you to feel better. Try it. Go for a bike ride, play catch, run, swim in the pool, jump on the trampoline, or do whatever kind of sport or exercise you enjoy.

3. REFLECTION
A million voices have access to you online, but **disconnecting** and being alone with no distractions allows you to develop a relationship with yourself. Find a quiet place where you can be alone to think. Sometimes you just need to have a conversation with yourself to work through things. Some people find writing in a journal extremely helpful. In a journal, you can be completely honest with yourself and let out your emotions. Other people find that sketching in a notebook helps them release and deal with emotions.

4. RELATIONSHIPS

Go spend time with someone you love. Talk to someone on your (team), or reach out to a friend. You might feel like talking it through with them, or maybe just being around them and doing something together, will make you feel better.

5. HIGHER POWER

When you are feeling bad, you can pray and ask Heavenly Father for help. Remember that you are **His child** and he wants to help you. Reading the scriptures can help you feel of His love for you. I keep a ring of notecards on my nightstand. When I find a really good scripture I write it down on one of the notecards. Then, when I'm having a hard day, I flip through these scriptures and find comfort. It's easy and you can do something like this, too.

6. HUGS

If you look at toddlers, you'll notice they all do the same thing when they are sad: they run to their mommas for a hug. That's because it really does make everyone feel better. So when you're feeling "meh," consider giving someone a hug, and make sure it lasts more than a second. (Your dog counts, too.)

7. NATURE

There is something magical about being in nature that makes you **feel better.** Go outside and enjoy the great outdoors. Take a walk, watch the sunset, climb a tree, fly a kite, go for a hike in the woods, lay down and watch the clouds, stargaze at night, plant a garden, pick some flowers, play with your pet, and so much more.

8. HOBBIES

What do you love to do? **Doing something you enjoy**

95

will help you feel better. Paint a picture, write a story, bake some cookies, read a book, shoot some baskets, build Legos, play Uno, put together a puzzle. If you don't think you have any hobbies, get creative. Learn something new.

9. SERVICE

One of the best ways to feel better about yourself is to **do something nice** for someone else. Who can you serve? It's even more fun when you do it in secret. Drop off a plate of cookies for your neighbor, empty the dishwasher for your mom, take out the trash, write a note to a friend, make your brother's bed, or play with your little sister.

Level Up!

1. What emotions do you think may trigger you to use technology inappropriately?

●

●

●

●

2. What is your action plan when you feel these emotions?

_____

_____

_____

_____

3. What do you like to do to "move your body"?

-
-
-
-

4. List three things you can do to get to know yourself.

-
-
-

5. Who is someone you can talk to when you are having a hard time?

_____

_____

_____

_____

6. What are things you can do to connect with Heavenly Father?

-
-
-
-

7. Who can you hug when you're having a bad day?

-
-
-
-

8. What do you like to do in nature?

-
-
-
-

9. Write down 3 hobbies you enjoy or would like to try.

-
-
-

10. Why do you think service makes you feel better? What are some things you can do to serve others?

_____
_____
_____
_____

Congrats! Now you have a bunch of things you can
do the next time you're feeling "meh"

Chapter 20:
When You Need to Make a U-Turn

"No one likes to fail...
but we mortals do not
become champions...
without making
mistakes."
— Dieter Uchtdorf [19]

WHOOPS

When I was 16, I picked up my friend to take her to a school dance. As we were nearing the school, we came to an intersection with a stop sign. We were running late (as always) and she told me to just run the stop sign. I knew it was against the law but I was also in a hurry to get to the dance, so I stupidly listened to my friend. Guess who was waiting to give me a ticket on the other side of the intersection? That $100 ticket was the best thing that could have happened to me as a new driver. I learned that rules are there for a reason and you can bet that I never gave into **peer pressure** again. It was a lesson I never forgot.

OWN IT

Just like I did, you might occasionally make poor choices as you learn to "drive" on your phone, but don't worry; there is **hope.** Your mistakes can actually be very helpful if you will use them as learning experiences. **Admit** when you've messed up and look for ways to improve. Don't live in denial or try to hide mistakes, because that will only make things worse.

Some of the mistakes you make might be simple to fix. Others might be more serious. You are not alone. You have been given the remarkable gift of repentance from **Jesus Christ.** As you turn to Him for help, you will be strengthened to do better. He has promised,

"I will show unto them their weakness...
My grace is sufficient for all those that
humble themselves before me; for if they
HUMBLE themselves before me and have faith
in me, then will I make WEAK things become
STRONG unto them."
-Ether 12:27 [20]

That's a pretty powerful promise. And the best part is that it's true.

You may make mistakes that are super embarrassing or make you feel terrible but please, please, please talk to your parents or a trusted adult on your team. **Don't suffer in silence.** Please don't ever think that the only solution to your problem is for you to hurt yourself. Your parents' love for you is greater than your mistakes. They will help you fix the problem. There is always hope.

Level Up!

1. Who can you turn to for help when you've made a mistake?

-
-
-
-

2. Why is admitting that you've made a mistake so important?

_____

_____

_____

_____

3. How can your mistakes help you grow?

_____

_____

_____

_____

Chapter 21:
#sharegoodness

"Let your light so shine before men, that they may see your good works and glorify your Father which is in heaven."
— Matthew 5:16

The world is at your fingertips! So how will you use your phone for good? Here are just a few ideas. Check the ones that you like!

- ☐ Be positive
- ☐ Study something new
- ☐ Listen to or read interesting talks, videos, and articles and share them with others
- ☐ Share inspiring quotes
- ☐ Post pictures of the beautiful world God created
- ☐ Send an encouraging message to a friend
- ☐ Index names off old records to use for Family History work
- ☐ Find your ancestors
- ☐ Text someone who needs love and support
- ☐ Communicate with faraway family members to strengthen relationships
- ☐ Share your testimony
- ☐ Organize a fundraiser

Show what you know about
#sharegoodness

1. What are some more ideas of positive ways to use technology?

-
-
-
-

2. Who is a good example to you of someone who uses technology for good? What does that person do?

_____

_____

_____

_____

Chapter 22:
Conclusion - You Got This!

And will you succeed? Yes! You will, indeed! (98 and 3/4% guaranteed.)
-Dr. Seuss

Congratulations! You did it! You just took the first steps in preparing yourself to "drive" on your phone.

Never forget that you are a **child of God.** He is aware of you and all of your struggles and He will help you. You have been sent here for a unique purpose. You will do amazing things. No one else can take your place. Remember that the Spirit will be your most important helper as you use your phone. You'll have to be disciplined and do hard things so that your phone can be a blessing and not a curse. Remember that you have an amazing team who loves you and wants you to succeed. You will make mistakes as you use technology, so don't forget to use the gift of repentance that Christ has made available to you.

As you use technology for good you will not only bless your life, but will be able to bless others around you. You got this! Now get on the road and start driving.

Smartphone Driver's Permit & Contract

By signing this Smartphone Driver's Contract you're saying:

"I have read through the Screen Ed "Driver's Education Manual," answered all the questions, and discussed the content with my parent(s). I understand that signing this contract means that I am working with my parent(s) as a team while I train in using a smartphone. I understand that my parent(s) will supervise and guide me as I practice "driving" on my device. My parent(s) have the right to take away my smartphone privilege if they feel I'm not using it appropriately in any way."

_____
Teenager's signature here

_____
Parent's signature here

Congratulations! You've earned your Smartphone "Driver's Permit" and are ready to start practicing!

Parents' Guide: How to Use This Book

Imagine if your 11-year-old asked you for the keys so she could drive the car. What would you say? What if she gave you arguments like, "Everyone else's parents are letting them drive and I'm the only one who can't!" You would think that was ludicrous! Most likely you would tell her that taking on that responsibility required learning and practice before she could safely drive a car. You would require her to complete a Driver's Education course where she could learn the laws that govern driving and the rules of the road that keep everyone safe. You would provide her with Driver's Training so she could practice making choices with the information she had learned but still with the watchful eye of an instructor who was there to give her feedback and tips on how to make sure she didn't injure herself or anyone else.

Now think of how many times your child asks you when she can get a smartphone.

Because the truth is **a smartphone has the potential to open the door to myriad dangers in young and inexperienced hands**-- dangers which include:

* Pornography exposure and addiction
* Increased rates of anxiety and depression
* Increased rates of suicide
* Phone use addiction
* Sleep deprivation
* Decreased empathy
* Decreased ability to navigate face-to-face social situations

Smartphones, tablets, and various social media apps became popular before anyone thought of how they could negatively affect us. Society has developed habits for use without guidelines or rules. No one has been trained in how to safely use smartphones because training has never existed. The device has been in control and not the user.

Parents and caregivers have a responsibility to teach their children how to wisely use this available technology-- which has the potential for so much good! This duty can feel overwhelming and scary. Many parents feel alone in this endeavor since very few have developed a way to manage this critical training. Filters and blockers on phone apps and computers are only part of the solution; they cannot catch everything. Parents have lacked a comprehensive resource to show kids how to navigate the issues safely.

Finally, a tool has been developed for teaching your child to be a wise technology user so you don't have to figure it out on your own!

Screen Ed: Your "Driver's Education" Manual for Smartphones, is the tool that teaches tweens and teens what they need to be ready to "drive" their smartphones. Just as you wouldn't give your car keys to your untrained teenager, smartphones should be used only after going through the training necessary to make wise and informed choices.

With this workbook, you can teach your child the **WHYs** and the **WHATs** for using technology wisely. You can provide your child with protective guidelines and principles. You can give your child the training necessary to avoid dangerous user "pitfalls" and the tools needed to overcome mistakes or wrong choices she/he will make.

HOW TO USE THIS BOOK
Screen Ed has 21 short chapters that cover many important aspects of smartphone use. Each chapter has a few questions at the end for your child to answer. The questions provide excellent talking points so that you, as a parent, can ensure that your child understands the main concepts in each chapter.

Some of the chapters cover sensitive issues like pornography and sexting. Screen Ed gives you a simple way to have difficult conversations and reduce shame surrounding these issues with your teen. Be open to these conversations as they arise. Your relationship with your child is your biggest tool and this workbook supports you in building that relationship. **Remember that if you don't talk to your teen about these issues, she or he will learn about them from someone else, often in terrible ways.**

Chapter 7 of the workbook contains **The Family Technology Plan**. Fill it out as a family and then post the tech plan in a place where it can be viewed often as a reminder of the smartphone user guidelines agreed upon.

Be sure to revisit the sections and the chapter-end questions periodically. Use this workbook as a reference manual that can be reviewed again, as needed, when various problems arise.

After completing this workbook and discussing the questions together, your teen will be better prepared to begin the journey of smartphone use.

-Jeannie Ondelacy Sprague, M.Ed.

Works Cited

1. Henley, W.E (1888). *Invictus*

2. Moses 1:3-6

3. Nelson, R.M. (2018, November). *Ensign*. Revelation for the church, revelation for our lives. © Intellectual Reserve, Inc.

4. Ephesians 6:17

5. Brandon, J. (2017, April 17). The surprising reason millenials check their phones 150 times a day. Retrieved from http://Inc.com

6. Oremus, W. (2017, November 10). Addiction for fun and profit. Retrieved from http://slate.com

7. Quick! Where's my phone? There's a human nearby. (2018, September 27). Retrieved from http://kaspersky.com

8. Natanson, H. (2017, June 5). Harvard rescinds acceptances for at least ten students for obscene memes. Retrieved from http://thecrimson.com

9. Napier, N. (2014, May 12). The myth of multitasking. Retrieved from http://psychologytoday.com

10. Castillo, M. (2012, August 8). Ohio teen hospitalized after playing video games for at least four straight days. Retrieved from http://cbsnews.com

11. Phillips, T. (2015, February 3). Chinese teen chops hand off to 'cure' internet addiction. Retrieved from http://telegraph.co.uk

12. Earl, J. (2016, January 8). Texas man posts message to cyberbullies after teen brother's suicide. Retrieved from http://cbsnews.com.

13. Anderson, M. (2018, September 27). *A majority of teens have experienced some form of cyberbullying*. Retrieved from http://pewinternet.org

14. *For the Strength of Youth*, (2011), p35 © Intellectual Reserve Inc.

15. Hinckley, G.B. (November 2004). Ensign. A tragic evil among us. © Intellectual Reserve Inc.

16. Ephesians 6:16

17. Zapal, H. (2019, April 9). Sate-by-state differences in sexting laws. Retrieved from http://bark.us
18. Keeping kids safe online. (2011, January 11). Retrieved from http://fbi.gov
19. Uchtdorf, D. F. (2013, November). Ensign. You can do it now. © Intellectual Reserve, Inc.

Amy Adams, MSW, PPSC

Amy holds Masters and Bachelors degrees in social work from UCLA and BYU respectively, and is a credentialed school social worker in California. She currently works as a middle school counselor. She is passionate about helping children and families navigate the digital world and establish healthy digital habits, which led her to be a co-founder of Healthy Screen Habits, a non profit organization. When Amy is not reading books about the interface of technology and culture she can be found playing board games with her husband and 4 children.

Made in the USA
San Bernardino, CA
29 January 2020